HOW TO BE A GOOD FATHER

PARENTING TIPS ON HOW TO BE THE BEST DAD

BY

DR DOUGLAS CARLA

TABLE OF CONTENT

INTRODUCTION;

□ DETAILED EXPLANATION OF FATHER

Fathers can support their child's growth by being a positive role model, engaging in play, and being a warm, caring parent. Being a father figure who shows a child love, support, and engagement, even if you're not the child's biological father, will be beneficial to the youngster.

Fathers have taken on three main roles throughout practically every culture that has been studied: protector, provider, and reprimander. Prior to going into detail about each of these duties, it is crucial to highlight that in many modern two-parent homes, mothers play each of these roles just as much as fathers.

Despite having different names, fathers are fundamentally the same. For a female, he is the prince charming she would always rely on because he is the first superhero we are aware of. It goes without saying that a father sacrifices everything for his kids and that he has an incomprehensible, unconditional love for them. He holds your finger when you need a helping hand because he loves without conditions. He follows closely behind to catch you if you fall and is always there to lend support and direction. A father can be many different things, but at his core, he is a devoted dad who will do anything for his kids.

CHAPTER 1

☐ SIGNS OF A GOOD FATHER

As mothers, we want nothing less than the best for our kids. We want to provide them with the best home imaginable, unconditional love, and most importantly, a solid, dependable family that includes wonderful parents who our kids can depend on at all times.

Even though mothers are typically the crazier of the two parents, one of the first questions we ask ourselves after learning that a pregnancy test is positive is whether or not our spouse is up for the challenge and even has what it takes to be a great father.

Here are several indicators that he'll make a wonderful father, so you don't need to worry.

1. He is tolerant

Even the most composed person can become agitated by children, but if your partner is patient, calm, willing to explain things several times, and doesn't lose his cool easily, that's a good place to start. He may occasionally lose his temper because he is only human, but that is to be expected.

2. He does not yell.

Even if he does lose it, he should ideally not shout. Young children find loud noises to be quite frightening, and they also detest it when their parents argue. Your man should be able to take a deep breath, say what needs to be said, and do so without raising his voice.

3. He has ambition.

He aspires to reach the highest possible levels in his career, as a husband, and as a father. Ambitious people strive for excellence in everything. Children imitate their parents, thus an ambitious father can really encourage your child and put him or her on a positive road for the rest of their lives.

4. He is assured

One quality that is impossible to teach, confidence is necessary for living a happy life. Yes, it's crucial that you have self-assurance as well, but the first few years of motherhood can be confusing. If your husband maintains his confidence at this point, your kids will infer it from him.

5. He assists with household chores.

He ought to! When you become a mother, you won't have as much time to clean up, so it's encouraging if your husband assists you now. He will undoubtedly need to assist you when the baby is born.

6. He looks after you when you're ill.

Men who have already become fathers can affirmatively state that when mom is ill, chaos reigns. He must be able to look after the young child and assist you in getting better. Because of this, it's unquestionably positive if he looks after you when you're ill right now. It is comparable to stretching before a major game.

7. He's a genuinely decent man.

When he notices a friend is having trouble, he will offer him a loan and assist an elderly woman cross the street. Some people think that being kind equates to being foolish, but I firmly believe that great fathers are great individuals.

Even though they wouldn't put anyone else above themselves or their family, they would always offer assistance when they could. Your man will be a fantastic father if he can walk that fine line. He will always treat you and your children well.

8. He wants a child.

Sometimes unexpected infants simply enter our life, and things work themselves out. Although it might be extremely nerve-wracking, it does require some time and work. It would be lot simpler for him to adjust to being a father if you and your man already wish to have a child.

9. He is dependable and adept at time management.

He keeps his word and returns home at the appointed time of six. He fixes things when you need him to. He always remembers to pay the bills on time. He can effectively manage his time and is accountable. To be a good father, you must possess it.

10. His sense of humor is good.

And ideally a lot of it. A strong sense of humor is always a plus, but when your infant grabs your phone and throws it across the room or you return home to a wall covered in drawings, you need to be able to laugh in order to survive. The child's ability to laugh is equally vital to his life.

11. He is adept with money

He'll also need a new phone, so the walls will need to be painted again.

12. He is gentle with kids.

How does he interact with the kids who must already be in your immediate area? Are they fond of him? Do they pelt him with rocks? If he's prepared to be a father, that's a fairly positive sign right there. If he isn't a fan of kids, don't become overly frantic; it's different when it's your child.

13.When he is hungry or hasn't slept for a while, he doesn't lose it.

Right now, taking care of the two of you occupies your entire universe. You eat when you're hungry. You sleep because you're tired. And while men don't have that, nature has made sure that the mother's body is programmed to go longer without eating or sleeping for the benefit of her baby's happiness (via hormones). Their wife suddenly takes priority, and when they are asked to help with the infant (frequently), they are unable to care for themselves. Yes, he'll have trouble sleeping well at night or eating exactly when he's hungry. I'm hoping he's able to handle such things now.

14. He accepts your refusal to have sex.

Some males are complete drama queens in the bedroom. "There are not enough of us." Is he one of them who says, "You're not really into it?" Because of this, you should let him know straight away that your sex life will suffer greatly. However, you should also make a commitment to him that after the baby is at least a few months old, you two will go on a vacation and catch up. He must recognize the end of the dark tunnel in order to stop losing his cool whenever you decline to have sex.

And it's even better if he doesn't have a temper tantrum.

15. He's useful.

You know you can always rely on him to fix something around the house because he has so many different tools? Great! You need a man like that when you have a child. He'll be the kind of dad that teaches his kids how to build doll houses and furnish them himself, in addition to being able to baby-proof your house and restore anything the kid has destroyed.

16. He already spends a lot of time at home

If your husband is a pity-monkey, you may have to endure endless evenings alone with the child while he is out "relaxing" after "a long day at work." If he enjoys spending time with you at home, it's a terrific indication that he'll make a good father; however, if he doesn't, you should sit him down and explain how things will work moving forward. Neither ifs or buts.

17. He is normally close to his family and takes good care of his parents.

With a man who doesn't appreciate family, how can you have a happy family? Not at all. Because of this, you ought to consider how close he is to his family and how well he looks after his parents. This will help you determine whether you'll be the one raising this family or your baby is set to have the best dad ever.

18. He is related.

What does being a father have to do with that? You're right that it's not a requirement, but siblings do teach you to be less egotistical. How to be considerate of other people's needs, even when you're a child and the world still revolves solely around you. How self-centered you are as a spouse relies on how self-centered your wife lets you be. Fatherhood makes it impossible to be selfish. Period.

19.He can cook.

It would be excellent if he could prepare a small meal for you two because you'll be occupied feeding your child or children. In any case, once you've put the infant to sleep,

20. He knows people who are parents.

Monkeys learn through doing. We unconsciously copy the habits of our social group because we believe them to be the proper ones. It's likely that he will be prepared to be a terrific father if he has friends who are fathers, preferably guys.

21.He's 30 or older.

Age is just a number, right? No, never. Men are kids before they get 30. They can be wonderful fathers, but it would be more challenging for them. After age 30, they are typically prepared for marriage, security, and the gift of life that a woman can provide.

22. He is amusing.

A child's development depends heavily on play, and other kids won't constantly be present. He likes playing with dogs, right? Has board game night ever occurred? Perhaps he enjoys playing catch? A terrific attribute for a dad is playfulness.

23. He can give severe love.

The most important thing that kids need is firm love. Ah, love. It's simple to allow children to veer off course, but the likelihood of this happening is much reduced if the child has a father who loves them while also having the ability to be firm with them.

24. He is encouraging.

Children have dreams. Big! They excel in it. And if their parents are encouraging, they begin to think that their goals can actually come true. That is the conviction that will keep them going through the darkest of times. Your spouse is in favor of all your illogical ideas? There you have a fantastic future father.

25.He doesn't feel disgusted for no reason.

Cleaning up after a newborn requires removing waste, urine, puke, and spit from... I suppose everywhere. You might not always feel like doing something. It's helpful to have a man in these situations who can assist rather than run away screaming.

26. He is a good teammate.

What exactly is a family? Nothing but a small group. To make a family function, you need a team player. to make being a parent work. When your child wants what he ought to have, you need to be on the same team. When he cries "bloody murder," you must be on the same team. You only have to stand on the same side.

27. He has faith

When you first have a child, you are constantly concerned that you might kill it by accident. Really, it's a requirement of the job. Because of this, you require a husband who respects your judgment and doesn't hover over you, offering suggestions or expressing concern at every turn. Does he believe you to make crucial decisions? Good.

28. He has a pastime.

A man who enjoys something will have a method to relax after a long day of raising children. Because occasionally watching TV while curled up on the couch just isn't cutting it. So that your mind can unwind from all those parenting thoughts and you can actually recharge, you'll need to focus on something you love to do.

29.He adores you.

Last but not least, having a child is the ultimate relationship test. Simply put, if you don't love each other, you won't be good parents. I thus hope he truly loves you for your sake and the sake of your child. And if that's the case, you know it in your heart.

CHAPTER 2;

◻ QUALITIES OF A GOOD HUSBAND

Let this list of characteristics serve as a guide for your marriage, family, and entire life.

1. Feeling

He treats you with the respect his wife demands. No matter how many years have passed, he still likes you, is fond of you, kisses and embraces you, and is sweet and romantic to you.

2. Individuality

He doesn't depend on his parents or your parents to take care of your family's requirements for food, shelter, and other necessities. He puts a lot of effort into giving you a place to call home.

3. Dynamism

He is trustworthy, independent, and adept at directing and pointing your family in the right direction. You understand that you will never be lost in life while you are with him.You are prepared to submit to him as his wife because of this. He serves as an excellent example for your kids as well.

4.Loyalty

He is not dishonest. He doesn't make advances to other ladies. He worries about losing you.

5.Love of oneself

Since you are confident in his independence, you don't need to worry about him. He loves you and your family as much as he loves himself. In order to always be there for you and your kids, he works hard to maintain his happiness and health.

6. Trust

He trusts that you can do it. He doesn't treat you like a dishonest person who shouldn't be trusted. Additionally, he confides in you with all of his assets, cash, and regular salary.

7. Knowledge

Regarding #6, he actually has faith in you since you are the one person he can truly trust. He made an attempt to get to know you. He is aware of your favorite color, song, dish, and location, as well as your attitude and every other detail about you. He is constantly curious to get to know you.

8. Reliability
He is open and truthful. You may put your trust in him since he does the same for you.

9. Recognition
He remembers to say "thank you." Even the little things you do for him are appreciated by him. And as a result, you are more motivated to love and serve him

since you understand that your efforts won't be in vain.

10. Patience

He is not readily enraged by you, your children, or other people. When there are issues or difficulties, he does not readily become upset. He is able to put up with discomfort or endure hardship because he understands that these are all simply tests that are meant to make him stronger rather than weaker.

11. Stability

He is tenacious and reliable. Until he realizes his goal for you and your family, he never gives up. Even when his numerous attempts fail, he doesn't become disheartened and he doesn't give up. No matter how challenging or how long it takes, he will keep working to give your family a better future.

12. Restraint

He has self-control. He has the self-control to refrain from vices such as overeating, intoxication, boredom, lust, and others.

13. Wisdom

He has the ability to tell right from wrong. He is not a simpleton who keeps committing wrongdoings like lying, cheating, being careless, and being lazy while thinking that things are OK.

14. Recognizing

He comprehends you. He is aware of himself. He speaks with understanding. He is aware of his decisions or choices. He is knowledgeable because he lives and breathes what he preaches.

15. Kindness

He cares about you, so he comprehends you. He senses your happiness, therefore he wants you to keep feeling that way. He is aware of your sorrow and suffering and wishes to take all possible measures to make things better for you.

16. Forgiveness

He doesn't seek revenge. He doesn't keep a record of your past errors or review them. He is capable of forgiving, forgetting, and moving on to live a happy life alongside you and your kids.

17. Holiness

He abhors wickedness. He leaves behind corruption, malice, and sin. He is fortunate because he acts appropriately and does the right thing. His moral deeds produce positive karma in your life and the lives of your kids.

18.Justice.

He is just and fair. He won't ever make you feel like life is so unfair having him in it.

19. Honor

As a woman, you have his respect. He respects your decisions and beliefs even if they differ from his. He is also capable of respecting himself.

20. Contentment

With you, he is pleased and joyful. You fulfill his fantasy for him. He has no desire to have additional spouses or mistresses. He never feels envious of other men because he believes that having you makes him the luckiest man alive.

21. Compassion

He understands sacrifice. Prior to thinking about himself, he considers you and your kids. He sacrifices things for you out of love. He does not just spend for himself but also for the rest of the family. You won't discover any justification for labeling him selfish.

22. Religion

He is a devout Christian. He abides by God's laws and puts His teachings into effect in daily life. He brings God closer to you and your children.

23. Hopefulness

Regardless of how challenging the present may be, he always envisions a bright future with you. He doesn't give up on you easily despite your flaws and faults. He always sends you wonderful energy that makes your house and family happier, more self-assured, and always perseveres no matter how challenging life is.

24. Reliability

He is devoted to you. He has faith in you. He can trust you without always seeing you. To be confident with you, he doesn't need to fully understand you. He demonstrates his faith by listening to you, showing you love, and making sacrifices for you.

25. Diligence

He gives his everything for you. He is driven to work hard to create a better future for your kids. He works tirelessly and passionately so that your family will always have food to eat and enjoy in the future. He doesn't waste time.

26. Generosity

He is a man of kindness. He is always eager to assist you and make you happy. He is not unkind. He doesn't intend to hurt you physically, mentally, or emotionally.

27. Mildness

He treats your body, mind, and heart with kindness. He corrects you when you make mistakes in a gentle, calm manner rather than angrily.

28. Peacefulness

He dislikes arguments and pointless conflicts. When you are not in a good mood, he doesn't argue with you. Whenever you require it, he provides you space and time. He chooses the ideal moment to speak with you and to listen so that you can both enjoy a restful night's sleep.

29. Humility

He is not haughty or conceited. His powerful mental, emotional, and spiritual makeup allows him to overcome pride and go low in order to uplift those around him and spread love, peace, and happiness.

30. Acceptance

You are accepted by him as you are. He does not condemn you. He doesn't try to make you into someone you're not. He still keeps motivating you to develop into a better person. By acting and modeling the change he wants you to be, he motivates you to make positive changes in your life.

31.Support

He encourages you in your efforts to develop into a stronger, more successful woman. He also encourages your kids to make their own decisions as long as those choices are moral and will make them truly happy.

32. Sincere love

And last, he really does love you. He is aware of it, is certain of it, feels it, and always expresses his actual feelings to you—even at inconvenient times and locations.

It could be challenging to locate a man who possesses the attributes of a good husband that I just outlined. However, a man will work to cultivate those traits if he is sincerely in love with a lady or his wife. Furthermore, isn't pure love what unites them all in perfect harmony?

☐ How to be a Good Husband and a better husband

Marriage is a lifetime commitment as well as a formal contract. In order to be with your spouse and cherish your love for as long as you live, you must make the commitment to do so when you get married. This commitment must come from the bottom of your heart and head.

Wedding vows are challenging to keep, it is a fact. Wearing your wedding band is a simple way to demonstrate your loyalty to your spouse, but maintaining that loyalty in your thoughts, actions, and heart is another matter together. Marriage involves acts and customs as well as symbols and ceremonies.

If you truly love your wife, you must demonstrate to her that you make every effort to be a decent and even better husband. Yes, it's simpler to say than to do. However, if you know what to do, you can start moving in that direction right away. Here are 30 tips to help you be a better husband if you have no idea how to improve your relationship with your wife.

1. Treat your wife the same way you treat yourself.

When you get married, your wife and you merge into one. Therefore, you should treat your wife with the same respect and affection that you would give to yourself. Do not harm your wife, and do not harm yourself.Keep in mind that if you can't love yourself, you can't love your wife. And if you can't even love your wife, how can you love yourself?

Therefore, if you love your wife, you should also love your body. Avoid being a glutton or an alcoholic. Avoid putting yourself in danger of illness and serious harm. Maintain a healthy way of living. Your wife will undoubtedly be pleased when you're well since she won't have to worry about you.

2. Savor the food she prepares.
You can eat the food she bakes or cooks as long as it is not harmful to your health or poisonous. You can be straightforward with her about the flavor; it will benefit her. But don't stop admiring her despite how it tastes.

3. Develop the skill of maintaining calm.
Love is tolerant. As a result, if you want to be a wonderful husband, practice patience daily. Learn to keep your cool under pressure and manage your anger. Be a grownup and the source of calm and serenity when others are arguing and fighting.

4. Be a great leader by being a great servant.

It's a man's responsibility to guide their own wives. But if you aren't trustworthy and reliable, how can you expect your wife to respect and obey you? So, prove to your wife that you are trustworthy. Prove to her that you are a trustworthy leader.

A trustworthy leader is one who leads through deeds, not just words. He isn't a bully. He sets an example for others to follow rather than just issuing orders.

5. Improve your son-in-law and brother-in-law roles.

Make your wife's parents and siblings pleased if you want to have a happier and more solid marriage. In order to maintain a peaceful connection with them as a member of their family, keep in mind that you have already joined their family.

What kind of a man are you if you love your wife but despise her family, if you are giving and nice to your wife but harsh to her family?

6. Put your pride aside.
Relations are ruined by pride. It damages your marriage's quality time and leads to small arguments. If you want to be a better husband, be a more modest person. Be the first to offer peace and ask for pardon, whether it was your fault or

hers. To raise your wife and your marriage, be practical.

7. Bear in mind crucial dates.
Remember her birthday, your wedding anniversary, and any other holidays that are significant to her. Along with remembering them, give your wife a surprise and cheer her up on that extremely special day.

Be dependable.
Do not ever lie. It's not just unethical; in certain nations, it's actually against the law. Keep your marriage promise, not just because you don't like to be imprisoned or be fined, but surely because you simply love your wife and

you want her to have a spouse who loves her and only her.

9. Concentrate entirely on her.

Even though it may be challenging, the eye is the body's lamp and is regarded as the doorway to the soul. Don't let your eyes sin, then, if you want to be the best husband to your wife. It might simply be your eyes that are transgressing now, but over time it might corrupt your soul as well.

10. Keep on courting her.

Despite how long you've been married to her, keep the romance and tenderness alive. Treat her like a princess or a queen by going on dates with her and sending her love letters. Focus on making her fall in love with you repeatedly rather than obsessing over whether she still loves you.

11. Show her respect.
Always show your wife respect. Do not forget that she is your wife. As a result, you should respect everything about her, including her rights and beliefs. You should also respect your connection with her and the fact that she is your children's mother. Even if you believe she doesn't deserve it, continue to show her respect.

12. Have faith in her.
Girls want guys to believe in them. They don't appreciate it when you have unfavorable thoughts about them. They don't want guys to view them as filthy

and unreliable. So, if you don't have any evidence that your wife is unreliable, just put your trust in her and stop feeling anxious or suspicious.

13. Pay attention to developing your credibility.

Focus on earning your wife's trust rather than having excessive doubts about her and becoming overly paranoid. Make an effort to convince her that you are a trustworthy person. Start by developing trust in your marriage from within.

14. Don't keep track of wrongdoing.

Has your wife ever made a mistake? When you fight, avoid bringing up such topics once more only to justify yourself. Leave the past behind, especially if you two have already made up with it and you have already extended her forgiveness. Bringing up old disputes only leads to unending debates.

15. Honor your love with reality.
When partners have nothing to conceal from one another, marriages are happier and healthier. Let the truth therefore win in your relationship. Always act in good faith and honesty. So that you can release yourself and carry on loving without holding onto lies, tell your significant secrets.

16. Give room and time.
When they are angry with you, some ladies prefer not to talk. If your girlfriend isn't interested in talking about a

problem in your relationship but you want to, don't push her to do so. Give her some room and time to gather her thoughts and to calm down. Be understanding and patient.

17. Acquire money-saving skills.
Put an end to overindulging in booze and meat. Put an end to vices like gambling and smoking. Stop making unnecessary purchases. To increase your income and wealth, put more effort into saving money. You can be sure that your wife and kids will be pleased.

18. Create your own house.
You need to have a place of your own. It's not necessary to construct a mansion, but a nice home—whether it's owned or

rented—that will grant your wife and you some freedom from your parents would undoubtedly help your marriage and family flourish.

19. Act as a good parent.
Mothers' love for their offspring is unadulterated. Be a good father first if you want to be a good husband. Giving your children everything they want or need is not the sole aspect of being a good parent. Teaching your kids the value of discipline is an essential part of being a good father. Set an example for them by exercising self-control.

20. Be giving.

Be willing to make sacrifices. Show your wife and kids that you are willing to make sacrifices for them. Relocate that business conference so you can see your daughter perform on stage at school. A romantic dinner date with your wife should take the place of that basketball game with your friends. So that you may always be there for your family, stay well and avoid being sick.

21. Show gratitude.

Be appreciative of the affection and attention your wife is showing you. Remind her of how stunning she is. Express to her your gratitude and gratitude for having her in your life. Get rid of whatever envy you may have. Do not evaluate your wife or your marriage in comparison to other couples. Be content and joyful.

22. Be gentle and kind.
You should treat your wife gently on all levels, including psychologically and emotionally. Most marriages feature opposing attitudes and lifestyles. Don't push or force your wife to change; it will just make things more difficult. Simply be nice and let her sense a welcoming atmosphere. You'll be astonished at how it influences a positive change in her.

If we're talking love and tenderness, don't make your wife have sex with you against her will. Even if she is married to you, it would be preferable if you could make sure that you both like it. If she's never in the mood, you'll need to go outside the box and come up with a plan to get her in the mood.

23. Get better at listening.

Avoid speaking too much. Listen to your wife more regularly to show that you are understand. Do something based on what you've heard to become a better husband. If your wife mentions any issues, assist her in resolving them. Give her whatever it is she asks for if you hear her asking. It's important to keep in mind that a good listener is also a doer.

24.Understand her.

What is her favorite shade, dish, blossom, location, film, or song? Why is she feeling so joyful or depressed? What are her aspirations for the future? What is it she wants you to develop into? To love her and bring happiness to her, you need to be aware of those things. Remember that wisdom is love.

25. Recognize her.

Feel her emotions, whether they are ones of joy or pain. Make sure she understands that you experience both happiness and sadness when she experiences either. Let her know that your hearts are linked and will always be together. Don't ruin her everyday pleasures. Join her even if it's awkward and she's out of pitch if she enjoys singing.

26. Keep her safe.

Be her champion. Protect her against threats that are not just physical but also mental, emotional, and even spiritual. In other words, avoid putting her under pressure, hurting her feelings, and exposing her to temptations. Bring her nearer to the Lord.

27. Encourage her.

She enjoys cooking and wants to open her own restaurant, right? Aid her in realizing her dream. Does she enjoy being a stay-at-home mother but become weary of looking after your home and kids? Give your wife a relaxing massage at night to help her unwind and recharge.

28. Have faith.

When you maintain your optimism for the future despite your current difficulties, you have hope. Don't simply hope; be hopeful if you want to be a better husband. In other words, be optimistic despite how challenging your current challenges may be. When your wife tries to change for the better, don't tell her she's hopeless. When you and your spouse are still working to keep your marriage together, don't declare it to be hopeless. Keep in mind that there is hope as long as you are alive.

29. Show loyalty.

Our hope is validated by faith. You should not only have hope, but also take steps to make your hope stronger if you want to make a terrific partner. Having hope without faith is hoping your wife will change without encouraging and motivating her. Additionally, being faithful does not mean that you refrain from lying and cheating in the hopes that your relationship would endure.

Do something to support your optimism; this is what being faithful entails.

30. Show her what real love is all about.
Last but not least, if you want to be a great husband to your wife, let her know what true love is like. By making an effort to adhere to the advice above, you can demonstrate your sincere love. Being a great or even simply a good husband is

incredibly difficult. But if you genuinely care about your wife, you'll be willing to make significant sacrifices to improve yourself and become a better man for both your wife and your kids.

The highest virtues of life, such as kindness, patience, compassion, gentleness, humility, and self-control, are produced when you love genuinely. Consequently, regardless of how challenging it is to be a great spouse, as long as you are genuine.

□ A Good Husband is a Good Father;

Ways to Be a Good Dad

Some people believe that men only have to take care of their children's necessities; mothers only have to raise the children. This is untrue, though. Dads must be actively involved in their children's life as well. As they get older, this will have a favorable effect on them.

So how can you become a good father? Here are some practical ways to do it if you're a new father still feeling your way around in the dark.

1. Provide for others well.
For improved financial security, most families nowadays already have both parents working. Make sure you are

doing your part well whether or not the mother of your children is employed.Your kids would undoubtedly appreciate it even if your pay is not too high as long as you are doing everything in your power to suit their demands.

2. Regularly spend time with your kids. Make the most of your children's youth while it lasts. When kids eventually have their own lives, you'll miss having them around. For this reason, find time to connect with them despite how busy you are at work. I appreciate one father who told me he spends thirty minutes a day with each of his children during a previous conversation.

3. Be there for them.

Don't go to your children's class recitals, graduations, or other important events unless they specifically invite you to. Be there for them whenever they need you, whether they are ill or just want to talk. It's critical that you are present for your kids to feel safe.

4. Lead by example.

Don't have vices like smoking and drinking alcohol if you don't want your kids to pick them up. Be a role model for them if you want them to be polite, diligent, and disciplined. The easiest method to teach your children is to demonstrate it for them.

5. Establish clear house rules.

Be tough and consistent with whatever house rules you establish, such as curfew hours, TV viewing restrictions, and chore allocations. Never give in to whims and justifications (unless valid). Apply corresponding penalties for breaking these regulations.For example, individuals who stay up past the curfew would be grounded all weekend.

6. Show them some patience.

It's common for kids to annoy you from time to time. However, do not lose patience with them despite how irritable they are making you feel. Never strike them out of rage because that constitutes physical abuse. Yes, I agree that spankings can be used as a form of discipline, but they must not be overdone, administered in a reasonable manner, and the purpose of the spanking must be made clear to the child.

7. Try not to be overly rigid.
Although the family needs to practice discipline, I don't believe being overly tough with your children would be beneficial. They may follow your orders today out of fear, but if they get the chance to be free, they will abandon the guidelines you have established. Many of my friends who had grown up in repressive families became incredibly emancipated.

8. Make them correct their errors.
It is your duty as a parent to ensure that your kids become morally upright and

upstanding adults. Don't be lazy in punishing them when they disobey, starting right now. For instance, if you catch them cussing, you must confront them right away, explaining why it is wrong and threatening punishment if you hear them do it again.

9. Learn to pay attention to them.
Parents may know better, but if you want to prevent your children from growing apart from you, learn to pay attention to their arguments. Despite the fact that you are the family's head, your kids have their own opinions. Let them first explain themselves before you ground them or reprimand them for something they did. If their justification

is invalid, you may then carry out the consequence.

10. Encourage them in their aspirations.
Allow your children to follow their passions rather than pressuring them to choose a career of your choosing. Encourage them to pursue a career or a college degree that speaks to them. They will be happier as a result, which will increase their chances of success in their chosen industries.

11. Let them make their own decisions.
Teach your children to be independent and discerning from a young age. They should acquire the ability to make decisions about what they desire, such as the meal to order or the style of shoes to

purchase. When they are older, they won't allow others to control them as readily.

12. Express your pride in them.

To your kids, it means a lot that you appreciate them as parents. Make sure they understand how pleased you are of them. Never compare them to other children and always express your appreciation for them in public. These will assist in enhancing their self-esteem.

13. Adore their mother

Loving and appreciating the mother of your children is one approach to being a good parent. Your kids might worry that your family would also disintegrate given the rising number of broken families in society. Showing children that your marriage is based on a solid foundation of love will help to protect them from this dread.

14. Assume the role of the family's spiritual head.

One of your main duties as the family's head is to encourage your children to follow the Lord. Set a good example for how to live a holy life. Take them through a time of family prayer and devotions. Make it a family tradition to attend church as well.

15.Man Up

Being a father is not always simple, and at times, the duties associated with the position can be burdensome. But for the sake of your loved ones, fortify your resolve, make plans for the future, and, with God's assistance and the support of your wife, work to be the greatest father you can be.

What Makes a Good Husband?

1. Individuality

2. Love

3. Loyalty

4. Self-love

5. Confidence in oneself

6. Appreciation

7. Spirituality

8. Integrity

9. Forgiveness

10. Righteousness

11. Contentment

12. Courage

13. Patience

14. Positive Influence

15. Self-control

16. Loyalty

17. Intelligence

18. Compassion

19. Sincere love

20. Dedication

CHAPTER 3;

□ PARENTING TIPS FOR DAD

Today's dads will likely tell you that their father-daughter or father-son interactions are very different from the ones they had with their own fathers. Men now have more alternatives for handling their responsibilities as dads, husbands, or partners because to changes in parenting practices. Today's father is less likely to naturally draw fatherhood advice from his own experiences as a child. What worked well for his father 30 years ago may not function at all with the numerous and various issues modern fathers face due to the continually evolving roles of dads.

According to recent studies, dads who are kind and accepting tend to raise their kids' self-esteem. Children's achievement, peer acceptance, and personal growth are all aided by a loving and compassionate father-child bond. Children's competency is aided by loving fathers who provide them fair but tough guidance without arbitrary imposition of their will.

1. Make time for your youngster.
What is important to a father is shown to his child by how he spends his time. Children develop quickly, so now is the perfect time to form close relationships. There are many enjoyable activities you can do as a family with kids.

2. Practice loving discipline and effective parenting.

All kids require loving supervision and discipline—not to punish, but to establish appropriate boundaries. Dads need to remind their kids of the repercussions of their choices and praise good behavior. Fathers who are patient and fair with their children's discipline are loving parents.

3.Set an example for your children.

Fathers serve as role models for their children, whether they are aware of it or not. A girl who spends time with a devoted father learns what qualities to search for in a spouse and grows up understanding she deserves to be treated with respect by boys. Fathers serve as role models for children, showing them what is important in life by being honest, humble, and responsible.

4. Work to earn your voice.
Fathers should start talking to their kids about significant issues when they're still very young so that they'll be able to manage challenging themes as they get older. Spend some time hearing the thoughts and worries of your youngster.

5. Teach your child by example.
Teach your kids what is right and wrong, and urge them to achieve their best, if you want to be a good father. Make sure your kids make wise decisions. Fathers who are actively involved teach their

children the fundamentals of life through common instances.

6. Share meals as a family.
Family dinners are a crucial component of a good family dynamic. It provides children with the opportunity to discuss their activities and future goals. Fathers should participate and listen during this time. It gives families a structure so they may spend time together every day.

7.Read aloud to your kid.
It is crucial for fathers to make the effort to read to their children in order to foster a lifetime love of reading in a modern society dominated by television and the internet. When they are very young, start reading to them, and as they get older,

encourage them to read independently. One of the best ways to guarantee kids will have a lifetime of literacy and personal and professional growth is to instill a love of reading in them.

8. Show respect to your child's other parents.

Children live in a safe atmosphere when their parents respect one another and show that respect to their kids. Children are more likely to feel accepted and appreciated within the father-child relationship when they observe their parents respecting one another.

9.Encourage participation early.

By learning about the responsibilities of a father through pregnancy, adoption, or surrogacy, you can express interest in your child at a young age. You can also gently touch, play, hold, and speak to an infant. When fathers are involved, they make the following very obvious and emphatic: "I wish to raise you as my own. We have a relationship that is significant to me and I am interested in you."

A man's life is drastically altered by becoming a father. Being entrusted with another person's responsibility and care is a huge responsibility, but few things are as fulfilling as becoming a father and watching your child develop gradually into an adult, receiving your love back in full measure and having their self-worth validated. Hopefully these parenting hints can offer some direction.

CHAPTER 4;

◻ THE RESPONSIBILITIES Of A FATHER: THE HOUSEHOLD HERO

The media hasn't really done a good job of portraying parents as being either awkward or completely unqualified to be a part of their children's lives, despite the current cliché.

Surprisingly, some males tend to be better parents than their mothers. We all think that it's a competition to make it more enjoyable, but it's not.

Remember that just because fathers are sometimes given a bad rap doesn't indicate that they lack the necessary parenting skills; otherwise, there would be absolutely no reason for a male to remain in a relationship after the child was born.

Fathers continue to have a significant role.

In addition to being a good father and spouse and offering equal amounts of support, a father's role also includes acting as a disciplinarian and helping to shape key areas of your child's character. This includes teaching youngsters about responsibility and recognizing right from wrong.

How To Be A Good Dad

1. Juggling enjoyment and discipline
Although there are benefits to enforcing rules, it's also important to strike a balance between rules and enjoyment.

You must understand that your children aren't automatons and that telling them repeatedly that what they're doing is wrong or harmful won't get their attention.

Knowing when to slow down and unwind is important. Being a completely autocratic parent never resulted in anything positive.

The best course of action is to be firm yet fair, as it is your responsibility to assist in developing your child's character.

Being a mother is challenging enough; you must play an equal role in your child's life as your wife does. Consequently, mothers cannot be everywhere at once.

The joys of parenthood include having fun with your young children and making them laugh and smile.

2. setting a good example
Despite occasionally claiming they don't like you or engaging in conflict with you, kids frequently emulate their parents.

Therefore, you must take good care of a very crucial aspect of your child's development: what you do in your day-to-day interactions with them.

One of your responsibilities as a father is to demonstrate to them how to remain composed under pressure, how to advocate for themselves, and how to respect others.

Your child's boy or girl will benefit from it, and it will play a significant role in determining how they develop in the future.

Your girls will seek those qualities in the partners they select for their foreseeable future partnerships. When they're older, your sons will use it as a reference on how to present themselves appropriately.

3. Taking care of the family

The reality remains that you should still contribute, even though traditional gender roles from the 20th century are long gone and households are becoming much more diverse, with the mother or even both parents filling the position of provider in some cases because the economy isn't particularly forgiving.

Because raising children is not exactly inexpensive, a good father is one who manages his finances well.

Spending tends to increase significantly when you have children. I should know because I buy clothes for my kids, and they grow out of their outfits really quickly.

And you should be concerned about more than just that.Food, games, literature, school supplies, extracurricular activities, tuition, and other expenses are also present.

Currently, it's crucial to earn money for the family in order to pay for all of these costs. This comes with a lot of responsibility and stress, which you men sometimes manage better than us women.

Again, the objective is not to spoil your children or to wallow in indulgence as a parent; rather, the objective is to provide for the necessities.

Your children will value having a financially responsible father who pays attention to them, demonstrates their importance and value, and who will do everything in his power to provide for their needs.

4. preserving a happy marriage (and other family bonds)
In addition to happy families, maintaining strong connections is the cornerstone of a good life in general. And yours ought to be the same.

Your interactions with each member of your home are equally as significant and crucial.

The relationship with your partner and making sure to always find common ground, especially during any potential disputes, are arguably the most relevant.

Putting a child through a divorce is the worst thing you can do to them.

You don't have to be an expert to understand how upsetting it can be for a youngster and the possibly catastrophic impact it can have on their development.

When we were in high school, a friend of mine went through one that had an effect on everything—her grades, her social life, her self-esteem, everything.

She became much quieter and more reclusive.

Thankfully, she was able to recover, but it took her a long time to get over having to choose between her parents. She felt responsible for the divorce and didn't want to interact with people for fear that she would lose some other connections that had ended for completely unrelated reasons.

Don't misunderstand me. It's not just your job to keep your marriage happy and bring up happy kids.

Modern parenting requires collaboration. The phrase "two to tango".
Maintaining and fostering respect and understanding between you and your partner is important.

Learn how to be adaptable and how to make concessions when a problem does occur.

It will have a negative impact on your kids.

5. Be a supportive parent and be available for your children.

You put in at least eight hours a day at your mentally difficult job as a father and try your best to support your family.

You don't have much time for yourself, let alone the rest of your family, on top of trying to keep a regular sleep routine and doing household chores.

All things considered, the same generally holds true for your spouse as well, but your children also require your attention and your presence.

Yes, if they stay at home, your spouse might get to spend more time with them, but children need their fathers just as much as their mothers.

Not to mention, she shouldn't manage everything by herself. When it comes to nocturnal diaper changes, bathing the infant, bottle-feeding, etc., both parents should alternate.

Even though you don't have much spare time already, try to get organized so you can spend time with your children.

Include kids in any tasks you may have, such as painting a fence, organizing the garage, and other similar tasks.

Start young; children as young as three and four may complete easy tasks. Heck, even a trip to the supermarket qualifies.

Or plan a weekend getaway in the countryside, take your young child to.

It doesn't always have to be about bonding over chores; it can also be about doing something enjoyable and relaxing.

It will give you two a chance to catch up on what has been going on in each other's lives and give you a chance to share your own perspective and advice on any dilemmas or situations they may be facing.

6. Do not mix up your relationships.
I don't intend for you to have an affair or do anything else with this, thank God.

What I mean is that you should keep your partner and children in separate relationships so that the children won't suffer if you ever get into a fight with your partner.

After all, it's they that matter.

This is particularly true in the case of a divorce, but it does occur more frequently than not in the US (God forbid).

If one parent abruptly withdraws from a child's life, it could be heartbreaking for them.

Do your best to prevent it from happening and make sure they are aware of your continued concern for them.

Avoid making them feel guilty.

7. assuming fatherly responsibilities
It all comes down to embracing the position that has been assigned to you in the end. I simply can't advise you to put up with it and be a decent parent.

No, you should acknowledge that you may occasionally make mistakes, but that's part of being human. You should also acknowledge that no two dads are alike and that each one has a unique approach to raising their own children.

There is no such thing as a perfect anything, and fathers are no different. However, it is a father's responsibility to be the best father he can be.

8. Think back to your own childhood. One thing I keep emphasizing is that your own experience can serve as your best instructor. The same holds true for future mothers and fathers.

Analyze how your father handled you in the past and draw lessons from it.

Learn what worked and what didn't so you may eliminate the bad and keep the things you think are good principles for raising your own child.

9. Talk to your children.

By communication, I don't just mean giving your son or daughter amusing nicknames and cracking jokes all the time. I also mean discussing "serious" topics with your children, even if it makes you uncomfortable.

Despite the fact that this relates to being there for your children, it's crucial for them to at least hear you, if only through a phone call, so they understand that occasionally you may not be able to do things due to commitments or health problems.

Instead of merely telling them "You're correct" and "You're an adult," it's much better for them to understand why some of your decisions were made.

They'll feel better about themselves and understand that you value them enough to take the time to explain things.

Responsibility is good, but...
Your body has limitations, whereas proper fatherhood has no boundaries. It can be difficult to keep up with everything.

Consider your health when making these decisions; not every home is the same.

Your life may be hectic due to additional commitments, greater work hours, illness, or the simple feeling of being overburdened with everything and needing a break.

You are not an exception to the norm that dads are also people.

Make sure you constantly have time to relax and take a load off since you simply won't be able to carry out the duties of a father at your best if you're not in good physical and mental health.

CHAPTER 5;

☐ Little Things That Mean a Lot to
Your Child

These straightforward things your children expect from you will reveal the art of being a good father to you. These seemingly insignificant events end up being the largest ones of all.

But first, a word of caution: You definitely don't need to complete everything on this list to be a wonderful father! For parents, this is a guilt-free zone.

Having said that, I'm sharing this list because I know how simple it is to get caught up in the daily grind and overlook these chances for genuine connection with our children. I am aware because I carry out my own. And because I value the contributions that excellent fathers make so much.

Find anything on this list that is either new to you or that you haven't done in a long, just for fun, and make it a personal goal to do it today.

1.Spend some time in the garage.
Bring your child along the next time you go to the garage to mend something or create something. Let them assist you after explaining what you're attempting to accomplish. Even if it could take you

longer to complete the task, you'll cheer up your child.

2. Join your kids in a dance.
Even if you can't dance, it doesn't matter. Jump up and down, spin in a circle, and sway from side to side. Play a fun family dance party playlist, then act silly. Along with being enjoyable, listening to music together strengthens family ties and forges wholesome memories.

3. Maintain a schedule.
Something you can do with your child every day—or at the absolute least, every week—together.

Every morning, my husband and our little child prepare a bowl of oatmeal and eat it together. You may have lunch dates with your kids, let them help you get dressed in the morning (by choosing your belt or socks, putting on your shoes, etc.), and wash your teeth at night as a family. The time and consistency of a shared ritual will be significant to your child, even if it isn't anything remarkable.

4. Submit inquiries.

This collection of endearing family discussion starters is one of my husband's go-to tools for teaching him how to be a good father. He uses it every night with our children. These insightful inquiries help everyone wind down the day.

Do not attempt to resolve a problem that your child brings up. Just listen to them chat; I know it's difficult. If you have to, you could try to gently prod them in the right way. But all they actually want is for you to listen.

5. Explain the laws.
Spend some time explaining the rules of the game to your child while you are watching your favorite athletic event on television. You'll most likely find a companion to watch the upcoming game with.

6. Leave voicemails.

If you send your child a card, include a heartfelt note with it. Your remarks, whether in a sentence or a paragraph, will mean the world to your child.

Surprise your child with notes in their lunchbox or Post-It notes on their bathroom mirror on regular days. You can make a joke, list your favorite qualities about them, or simply express your affection.

7.Read out loud.
Reading to your child is never too old. Give younger children a bedtime story to read. You can alternate reading aloud from the same book to older children.

8. Go on a date for coffee.

Bring your favorite card or board game to the local coffee shop, then treat yourself and your kid to a luxury beverage while you play — coffee for you, hot chocolate for them. Here is a list of our top favorite board games for families of all ages, many of which we still play today.

9. Astonish your children.

One day, even a half-hour early, leave work and head home. Or, even if it's just once a year, take the day or the morning off from work to do something enjoyable with your children.

10. Trade off on who writes.

Get a shared journal so that parents and children can correspond with one another. This is my favorite father-daughter or father-son notebook since it provides a magical trick for getting your child to open up so you can keep in touch. Alternatively, this dad and I art notebook works excellent if you'd like to share a drawing diary.

11. Take the kids with you to work.

At least once, do it. Show them your workspace, the coffee maker, and the conference room where you struggle to remain awake during your weekly status meetings. Inform them of your daily activities when you are not with them.

12. Make a strong statement.

Say it out loud frequently to your child to remind them of your unwavering love. You can tell them, "You are significant to me," "I feel very fortunate to be your father," or simply, "I adore you."

13. Related tales.
Simple tales from when you were young are quite popular with your youngsters. Additionally, share tales from when they were kids.

14. Step outdoors.
When you get home from work, I know you'll be exhausted, but gather the kids and head outside. All you need is a few minutes. I'll wait till dinner, I swear. Uncertain of what to do? Play catch, seek for fascinating bugs, go for a fast bike

ride around the block, or get on your bikes.

15. Prepare supper.

Pick a night and prepare supper with the kids, whether you are the family chef or your partner does it more often. Include them in the process of choosing what to produce, then include them in the actual production of it. (Plus, they'll be much more inclined to consume a meal they assisted in preparing.)

16. Pause to play.

Your child will cheer when you take a seat and play for a while without using your phone or doing anything else at the same time.

16. Crack jokes.

These two joke books are our faves if you don't know many family-friendly jokes, and they're both very affordable: Kids' Knock-Knock Jokes and Laugh-Out-Loud Jokes. (If you enjoy those, this author's many joke books include a ton of suggestions.)

18. Start a pillow fight or roughhousing.

According to research, this type of play makes kids happy, including girls, and develops their emotional intelligence.

19. Express thankfulness.

Look your child in the eye and say "thank you" when they do something kind or remember to do something you always have to remind them to.

20. Browse pictures.

Sit down and go through the family photos, whether you have a physical photo album or a folder of images on your computer. Remember enjoyable family trips, your children's first steps, and birthday celebrations.

21. Participate in a team sport.
Try playing some basketball or tennis, or just catch.

22. Accept it.
Say "yes" when you normally say "no" to your child's surprise. Can I have some chocolate please? Yes! Possibly a game? Yes! Can you instruct me in driving? Uhh...yes?

23.apologize

It doesn't make you a "weak" parent if you apologize to your child. It takes courage to apologize since doing so teaches your child how to be a kind, considerate person.

If you got angry and shouted at your child, apologize to them and promise to do better going forward. Ask them if they'll repeat themselves if they were trying to tell you anything but you weren't listening. If you made a commitment to them and were unable to fulfill it, explain how you intend to make it up to them.

24. Be there.

Attend your child's performances, sporting events, dancing recitals, and science fairs. Be there, whatever their pastimes or interests may be.

25. Hug.

You can never have too many hugs from your father. Make sure they last six seconds or longer and are of high quality. This is why. Try high-fives if your kids are older and less receptive to hugs.

CHAPTER 6;

□ THE IMPORTANCE OF A FATHER IN A CHILD'S LIFE

Being a dad takes a lifetime, yet anyone can father a child. Every child's father fills a unique function in their lives that cannot be filled by anyone else. A child's experience in this job can have a significant impact on them and help mold them into the people they become.

Fathers and Children's Emotional Growth

Like mothers, fathers play a crucial role in a child's emotional growth. Children look to their fathers to establish and uphold the norms. Additionally, they look to their fathers to give them an emotional and physical sense of security. Children desire to please their fathers, and a supportive father encourages personal development and strength. According to studies, a child's cognitive development is significantly impacted by his or her father's affection and support.Additionally, it fosters a sense of general wellbeing and self-assurance.

The Standard for Relationships with Others is Set by Fathers

Fathers not only shape who we are on the inside, but also how we interact with others as we mature. The way a parent raises his child will affect the qualities the child values in others. Depending on how the youngster interpreted the significance of his or her relationship with their father, friends, partners, and spouses will all be made. The patterns a parent establishes in his interactions with his kids will determine how they interact with others.

Girls and Their Fathers

Fathers provide stability and emotional support for young girls. A father demonstrates to his daughter what a good man-woman relationship looks like. If a father is kind and kind, his daughter will seek out men who share those traits when she is old enough to start dating. She will connect with males of similar temperament intimately if her father is powerful and brave.

Sons and Their Fathers

Boys take after their fathers' personalities, unlike girls who take after the relationships they have with other people. From a very young age, boys will look to their fathers for approval. Humans learn to function in the environment by modeling the conduct of others around us as they grow up. If a father is kind and respectful toward others, the young son will develop in a similar manner. Boys look to other male role models when their father isn't around to set the "rules" on how to act and thrive in the outside world.

Don't forget to tell your dad today how much you appreciate him and how much you adore him!

CHAPTER 7;

□ Practical advice that can help fathers.

1. Make Family Time a Priority.

How can a father demonstrate to his kids that they are important to him? You undoubtedly go above and beyond for your kids, making sacrifices to feed them and give them a decent place to live among many other things. If your children were not essential to you, you would not act in such a way. However, if you don't spend a lot of time with your kids, they can assume that you are more concerned with other things like your career, friends, or interests than you are with them.

When should a father start hanging out with his kids? Even while the infant is still in the womb, a mother and child start to develop a relationship. After 16 weeks of pregnancy, a baby may start to hear. At this point, a father can begin to develop his own special bond with his unborn kid. He is able to communicate, sing, feel the baby kick, and listen to its heartbeat.

2. Good Fathers Communicate Well

Listen objectively without passing judgment.

You must pay close attention to what your children are saying in order to communicate with them effectively. You must learn to listen without jumping to conclusions.

Your kids won't be as inclined to talk to you about their inner thoughts if they believe that you would snap at them and be critical. However, if you patiently listen to them, you'll come across as someone who is genuinely interested in them. They will also be far more willing to open up to you and express their deeply personal feelings.

3. Distribute kind correction and praise
Even when you're upset or angry, the punishment you give your child should come from a place of love and care for

their long-term welfare. Advice, correction, instruction, and reprimand as necessary are all included.

4. Respect and Love Your Wife

Children will undoubtedly be impacted by a father's actions in his capacity as a husband. "One of the nicest things a man can do for his children is to appreciate their mother," a group of child development experts says. "A father and mother who respect each other and let their children know it produces a secure atmosphere for them.

5. Use God's Useful Wisdom
Fathers who genuinely love God can bestow upon their offspring the most

priceless inheritance: a close relationship with their heavenly Father.

It is evident that parenting entails more than just five elements, and that even when you put forth your best effort to be a good father, you won't be.

But you can be a good parent if you use these guidelines in a caring and sensible manner.

CHAPTER 8
▢ WAYS TO BE A BETTER FATHER RIGHT NOW

There are many duties that come with being a father, most of which cannot be delegated to another person. The majority of men want to be the best fathers they can be, but nobody has ever explicitly told them how to accomplish it. Most of what we discovered about fatherhood came from observing our own parents. Unfortunately, a lot of us have never taken the time to reflect on what we have learnt. We don't have much time for introspection as we go about our daily lives taking care of business.

1: Put your phone aside when you are around your children.

When you're with them, be present and leave anything related to work or pleasure, like your cell phone, at home. Emails and social media are highly alluring, but our children need our attention more than any of that. You'll be astounded at how amazing it is to simply be with your kids and take in their existence. Watch them for a bit, and then cherish the memory because they really do grow up quickly. Don't look back on the time you spent raising your children and wish you had spent more time with them or feel guilty for not using it as effectively as possible.

Men are predisposed to become preoccupied with their profession. It can be simple to leave the house in the morning and work or hang out with the men for as long as feasible. We make the assumption that our children are safe at school or at home with the other parent, and they are. Fathers must keep in mind that their children depend on them as well. Whether it's during supper, bath time, or bedtime, make sure to spend some time with your kids each day.

2: Be a positive role model for your children.

It's simple to tell your children one thing while doing differently.

Just keep in mind that children follow our example and not our words. Be a nice person in every way and a parent they can look up to if you want your children to grow up to be well-adjusted, responsible, and moral individuals.

Because every man is different in that regard, it is up to each individual to evaluate themselves and determine where they need to develop. If you become angry, refrain from swearing or throwing objects. Be gracious to everyone you encounter. Donate to worthy charities. Allow your children to see you reading a book rather than vegging out in front of the TV. Make dinner, wash the dishes, or take out the garbage as you step up your game around the house.

Without you having to sit down and lecture them, being a father whom your children can look up to will teach them a great deal about what it means to be a man. Even if you did exactly that, kids often pick up on our character when we least expect it, so just assume that they are constantly watching you and provide them a role model for their father.

3. Set aside one date per week; your kids will appreciate it.

Decide to schedule a date once per week. Your children will miss out on some time, but it will be worth it when they understand that their parents love them.Learn to be a giving man and to appreciate your partner. Make life as simple as possible for your partner, whether that means running to the store after work or bathing the kids so they can relax after a busy day.

Nothing gives children the sense of security that a close-knit family can. Even the most romantic of relationships can rapidly become strained by issues with money, children, health, and other life concerns. With everything going on, it's simple to start drifting apart from your partner. Stop that from happening.

Make a list of 10 things about your significant other for which you are grateful if you want to rekindle your love for them. You might even make a personalized note out of the list and set it on the person's pillow or refrigerator as a surprise.

4. Heal the hurts from your past. Don't make them suffer so that your kids can.

Many of us unintentionally repeat the past when we treat our children the same way our parents treated us. These interactions can sometimes be advantageous. Perhaps your father read you a particular book, and every time you read the same book to your child, you are transported back to that unique experience.

However, some things aren't so good. We frequently act out these situations with our kids in an effort to mend our own inner wounds. Examine your responses to your children's misbehavior.Are there any words you use or things you do that bring to mind an event from when you were younger? You'll be shocked at how many unintentional parenting errors we pass on to the following generation.

Additionally, you might set internal standards for your children, such as excellence in school, talent in sports, or artistic ability. Do you have the same expectations for yourself from your parents? Consider your own upbringing by doing some soul-searching. Keep the positive aspects and impart them to your kids. Recognize the negative aspects, but instead of taking them out on your children, try to heal them through counseling or spiritual interests.

5: Don't share too much with your children.

Sharing our adult concerns with our kids is not appropriate, and expecting them to support us through them is even less so. Every man will, in all likelihood, experience difficulties in life. You can be struggling to make ends meet, deal with problems at work or home, or even with your spouse or parents. Find a constructive outlet for your stress, and talk to the appropriate people about it. Do not argue in front of your children if you and your spouse must. Postpone it till later. The future? You might even stop needing to debate.

Leave any issues you are having at work; do not bring them home. It can be quite challenging to categorize our life into small boxes, but allow yourself to be inspired by the knowledge that verbal abuse such as yelling and bickering can be far more harmful to your children than it is to you. Being a rock-solid, trustworthy family member who they can rely on and feel secure around is a crucial component of being a man and a father. It's acceptable to have problems; just learn when and how to communicate them to the appropriate parties.

6: Learn about your children.

Do you know what type of ice cream your child prefers? Do you know what their preferred read or watch is? Do you know their favorite genres of music?

The majority of us don't actually consider what matters to our children. We glance at them from time to time, but we hardly ever interact with them to learn more about who they are. Don't lose out on their young world or their perspective on the world as they get older. Kids misbehave a lot because they seek their parents' attention or because they believe they are not understood by them.

You'll be astounded at how spending time with your children doing the activities they enjoy helps improve communication and reduce many problematic behaviors. Are your kids basketball fans? Visit a basketball game with them. Are tea parties something they enjoy? Get on the ground, sip Earl Grey, and eat biscuits while acting. You won't feel bad about skipping a football game in the future. If you don't get to know your kids, you will regret it.

Making time for your children helps them grow up happier and better adjusted, which translates to your children developing more positive relationships throughout their life. Checked-out parents frequently witness their children leaving without turning around to look.

7: Don't hold your children to unreasonable standards.

It is reasonable to demand of your children that they behave responsibly, complete their tasks, give their all in class, and respect other children and adults. After all, you want your children to develop into happy, well-adjusted adults since it will make them successful in life as well as make you happy.

However, expecting your children to live up to your unrealized aspirations of being a rock star, a professional athlete, or a master of chess is unfair. Allow your young children to try out various things when they are young, whether it be karate, soccer, art class, ballet, or anything else. Let them pursue anything they have interest in and enjoy it.

You won't be able to coerce your children into doing anything when they are older. No matter how wacky it might appear to you, just show interest in whatever they find interesting. Maintain fair expectations for them, such as having them complete their homework, their chores, and showing respect. But don't feel bitter within about them not following their aspirations.

8. Take your time with your children.

Having patience with children of any age is difficult. When children are young, they become upset over the silliest things. When they get older, they'll test the boundaries and go beyond what is acceptable in ways that can cause you to get more gray hairs.

Keep in mind that children are children. They are still learning how to behave, so we must do our best to support them when they unavoidably mess us up. Expect the unexpected when they learn how to mature and function as an adult because they are still growing up. Ironically, a parent who constantly yells at their child or threatens them with punishment may discover that their children continue to misbehave.

Kids frequently appreciate the passion and effort adults expend in responding to their pranks. It is attention, after all. Just be aware that children will mark the wall with paint. They'll smear applesauce all over your clothes. They'll stay out later than you prefer. You won't like the clothes they bring back from the mall. Whatever the circumstances may be for your child, simply be aware of everything in advance to reduce your tension. Your kids will see a positive example of how to deal with obstacles in life, and you'll be happier and healthier.

9: Schedule some alone time.

When you don't take time for yourself, it's difficult to be your best self. You won't be able to use any of the advice we've provided above if you're overextended. So, make sure you're looking after yourself. When we have children, it might be simple to become mired in life's details and overlook the little things that make

Make sure to set aside time to take care of yourself. In the morning, take a hot shower and dress in fresh clothing. Have a nutritious breakfast. On the way home from work, pause at a park and stroll around for ten minutes. Make sure you spend time with friends engaging in fun activities every so often, possibly weekly or monthly. And don't forget to share this self-care with your partner so they may obtain what they require as well.

The process of raising children can cause many parents to lose their identities. Keep up with the hobbies and interests you have, whether they are music, sports, or reading about the past. You might even discover that your children desire to join as they get older.

CONCLUSION;

☐ Final word

Fatherhood is a lifetime experience that we pass on to our children when they grow up and become parents. You won't regret making the effort to improve your relationship with your children and turn out to be the father they deserve, even though being a good father demands a lot of self-control and personal development. When you make a mistake, don't be too hard on yourself; mistakes happen to everyone. You're doing honorably as long as you're trying your best to be a decent father.

How to Reconnect With Your Child After a Difficult Situation

In order to bridge the gap between you and your child after a bad interaction, you should reconnect with them for a few happy moments.

Because if you don't bridge that gap and your child feels disconnected from you, that will result in more pointless power battles and less cooperation on your part when you ask them to do something.

Unfortunately, it's really challenging to come up with a nice and entertaining activity to perform with your child so you can bond while your brain is currently overflowing with stress chemicals.